Reading/Writing Companion

Mc Graw Hill

mheducation.com/prek-12

Copyright © 2023 McGraw Hill

All rights reserved. No part of this publication may be
reproduced or distributed in any form or by any means,
or stored in a database or retrieval system, without the
prior written consent of McGraw Hill, including, but not
limited to, network storage or transmission, or broadcast
for distance learning.

Send all inquiries to:
McGraw Hill
1325 Avenue of the Americas
New York, NY 10019

ISBN: 978-1-26-572620-1
MHID: 1-26-572620-5

Printed in the United States of America.

3 4 5 6 7 8 9 LMN 26 25 24 23 22   A

Welcome to WONDERS!

We are so excited about how much you will learn and grow this year! We're here to help you set goals for your learning.

You will build on what you already know and learn new things every day.

You will read a lot of fun stories and interesting texts on different topics.

You will write about the texts you read. You will also write texts of your own. You will do research as well.

You will explore new ideas by reading different texts.

Each week, we will set goals on the My Goals page. Here is an example:

I can read and understand realistic fiction.

I've never read realistic fiction. I'll shade the **first box**.

I want some more practice with realistic fiction, so I'll shade the first **two boxes**.

I can read and understand realistic fiction. I'll shade in **three boxes**.

I've read a lot of realistic fiction and I like to share what I know. I'll shade all **four boxes**.

As you read and write, you will learn skills and strategies to help you reach your goals.

You will think about your learning and sometimes fill in a bar to show your progress.

Check In 1 2 3 4

Here are some questions you can ask yourself.

- Did I understand the task?
- Was it easy?
- Was it hard?
- What made it hard?

It is okay if I need more practice. The most important thing is to do my best and keep learning!

If you need more support, you can choose what to do.

- Talk to a friend or teacher.
- Use an Anchor Chart.
- Choose a center activity.

At the end of each week, you will complete a fun task to show what you have learned.

Then you will return to your My Goals page and think about your learning.

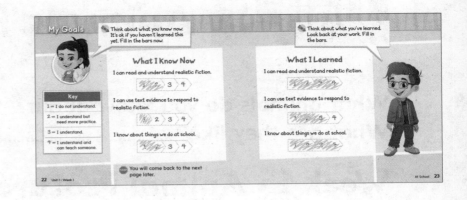

Unit 4 Animals Everywhere

The Big Idea

What animals do you know about?

Week 1 • Animal Features

 Digital Tools Find this eBook and other resources at: **my.mheducation.com**

Week 2 • Animals Together

SCIENCE

Georgette Douwma/Stone/Getty Images

Week 3 • In the Wild

Week 4 • Insects!

Week 5 • Working With Animals

Extended Writing

Poetry

Connect and Reflect

Animals Everywhere

Listen to and think about the poem "Animals on the Go."

 Talk about other animals you know. How do they move?

The Big Idea

What animals do you know about?
What are they like?

Build Knowledge

Build Vocabulary

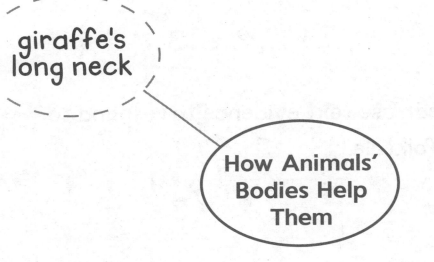

Talk with your partner about animals you know. How do their bodies help them?

Write words about how those animals' bodies can help them.

giraffe's
long neck

How Animals'
Bodies Help
Them

My Goals

Think about what you know now. It's important to keep learning. Fill in the bars.

What I Know Now

I can read and understand a folktale.

1   2   3   4

I can use text evidence to respond to a folktale.

1   2   3   4

I know about ways animals' bodies can help them.

1   2   3   4

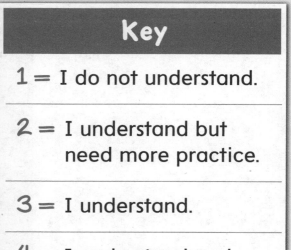

Key	
1 =	I do not understand.
2 =	I understand but need more practice.
3 =	I understand.
4 =	I understand and can teach someone.

 You will come back to the next page later.

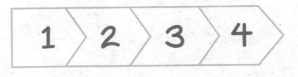

Think about what you've learned.
Keep working hard! Fill in the bars.

What I Learned

I can read and understand a folktale.

1 > 2 > 3 > 4

I can use text evidence to respond to a folktale.

1 > 2 > 3 > 4

I know about ways animals' bodies can help them.

1 > 2 > 3 > 4

Shared Read

My Goal
I can read and understand a folktale.

 Find Text Evidence

 Think of a question about the story. Use the title and illustration to help you. Read to find the answer.

 Circle and read aloud the word with the long *a* sound spelled *ai*.

Essential Question

? How do animals' bodies help them?

Snail and Frog Race

Shared Read

🔍 Find Text Evidence

Underline and read aloud the words *about* and *our*.

Circle and read aloud the words with the long *a* sound spelled *ay*.

This is a tale about Frog and Snail. One **splendid** day, Snail sat in the grass. Just then, Frog hopped past.

"Let's play!" said Snail.
"Yay!" said Frog. "Let's race to our school."

"Yes," said Snail. "To win, we must get inside the gate."

🔍 **Find Text Evidence**

Ask any questions you may have about the text. Read to find the answer.

Underline and read aloud the words *animal*, *give*, and *carry*.

Snail was not a fast animal. He inched his way along the trail. Then Frog hopped past, fast, fast, fast!

"I will give you a tip," yelled Frog. "Hop like me. And don't carry that big shell!"

"I can't hop. I don't have long legs," said Snail. "And this shell is home."

🔍 **Find Text Evidence**

Ask any questions you may have about the text. Read to find the answer.

Talk about Frog. How did she get to the gate first?

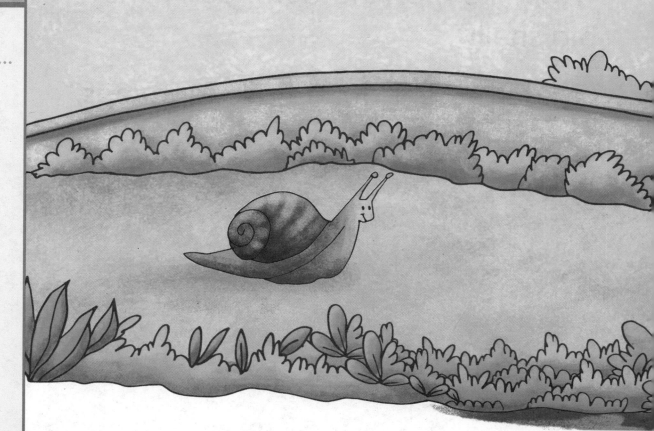

"I will win, then!" yelled Frog. "At this rate, it will take you eight days!"

Frog hopped past, fast, fast, fast! Snail inched along the trail.

Then Frog came to the gate.
"I made it," she bragged.
But the gate was locked!
Frog hopped up. But the gate
was too big.

Shared Read

🔍 **Find Text Evidence**

Ask any other questions you have about the story. Then retell the story to find the answers.

Frog sat and waited for Snail.
At last, Snail came.
"I can't get in!" wailed Frog.

Snail used his **special** sticky body
to slide past the gate.
"I win!" said Snail. Then he rested.
It had been a big day.

Write Sentences

 Talk about how Snail worked hard.

 Listen to sentences about working hard.

John and I did it! We finished our science project on Orion. We won third prize!

 Talk about the topic.

 Underline descriptive words.

Writing Traits

- Remember to focus on **one topic** in your writing.

- **Descriptive words** tell more about something or someone.

Talk about a time you worked hard.

Write sentences about a time you worked hard. Use descriptive words. Make sure you focus on one topic.

_____

_____

_____

_____

_____

Talk about the topic of your writing.

Underline descriptive words in your writing.

Check In 1 2 3 4

Vocabulary

 Listen to the sentences and look at the photos.

 Talk about the words.

 Write your own sentence using each word.

special

Penguins move in a **special** way.

_____

- - - - - - - - - - - - - - - - - -

_____

splendid

A peacock has a **splendid** tail.

_____

- - - - - - - - - - - - - - - - - -

_____

If you don't know the meaning of a word, you can use a dictionary to learn its meaning.

Find Text Evidence

I'm not sure what *bragged* means. I will use a dictionary to look up *brag*, the base word of *bragged*. I learn that *brag* means "to talk about yourself in a proud manner."

Then Frog came to the gate. "I made it," she bragged.

Your Turn

Use a dictionary to find the meaning of *wailed* on page 22. Write the meaning.

_____

_____

_____

_____

_____

_____

_____

_____

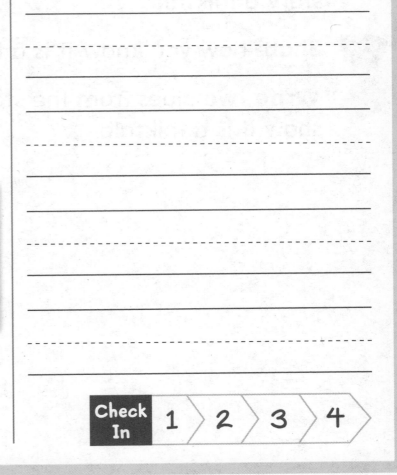

Check In 1 2 3 4

A **folktale** is a story that has been told for many years. Folktales may have animal characters that act like humans.

 Reread to find out what makes this story a folktale.

Share how you know it is a folktale.

Write two clues from the story that show it is a folktale.

Check In 1 2 3 4

Animal Character	How the Character Acts Like a Human

Shared Read

The **sequence** of events is the order in which the events appear in a story. The sequence of events is what happens first, next, then, and last in a story.

  Reread "Snail and Frog Race."

Use sequence words to talk about the events in the story.

Write about what happens first, next, then, and last.

Check In 1 2 3 4

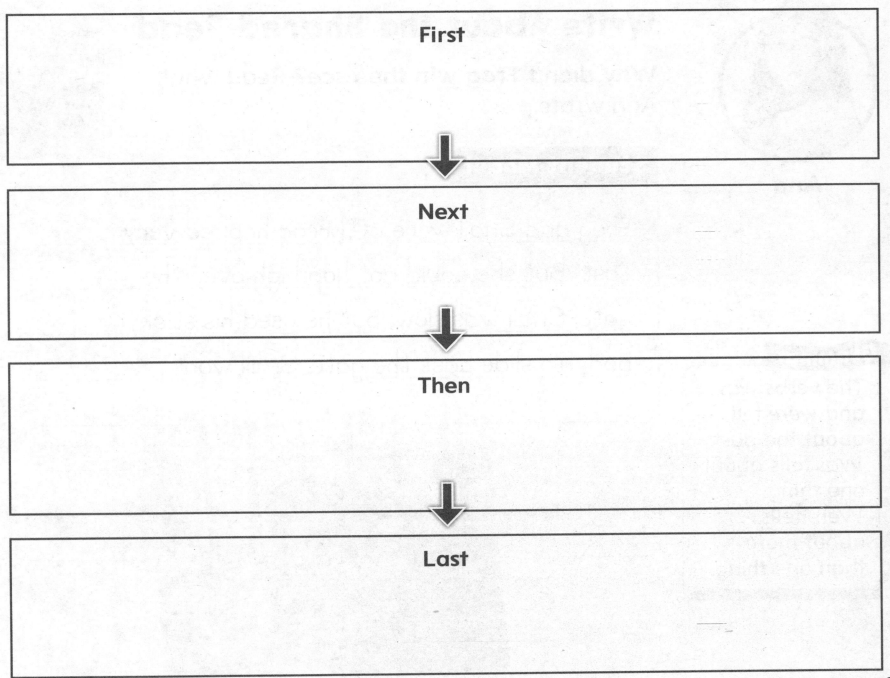

First

Next

Then

Last

Writing and Grammar

Ana

Write About the Shared Read

Why didn't Frog win the race? Read what Ana wrote.

Student Model

Frog and Snail were off! Frog hopped very fast. But she could not hop high over the gate! Snail was slow, but he used his sticky body to slide past the gate. Snail won!

Grammar

The verbs *was* and *were* tell about the past. *Was* tells about one thing. *Were* tells about more than one thing.

Talk about details Ana used from the story. Underline the descriptive words.

 Circle the words *was* and *were*.

 Talk about the topic.

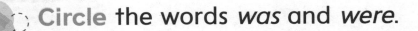 **Write** what you notice about Ana's writing.

Quick Tip

You can talk about Ana's writing using these sentence starters:

I noticed . . .
Ana used . . .

Retell the story in your own words.

Write about the story.

Why did Little Rabbit believe that the forest was falling?

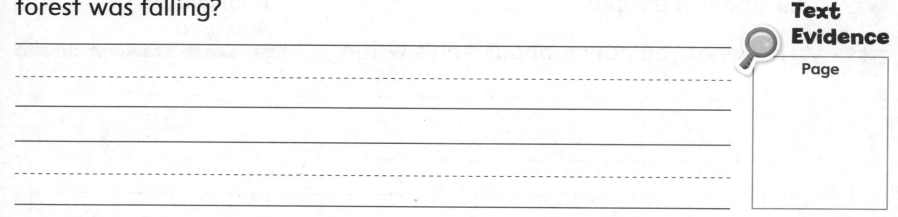

Text Evidence

Page

How were Lion's actions different than those of the other animals?

Text Evidence

Page

Check In   1   2   3   4

Talk about the illustrations on pages 13 and 15. How is Little Rabbit feeling?

 Write clues from the illustration that help you answer the question.

On page 13 Little Rabbit looks:	
On page 15 Little Rabbit looks:	

How do the illustrations help you know how Little Rabbit is feeling?

_____

_____

_____

 Talk about what the animals are doing on pages 16–19.

 Write about what each animal does after it sees the other animals.

What does Deer do?	What do Ox and Tiger do?

How does the author show how the news about the forest spreads?

_____

_____

_____

Talk about the events on pages 24–26. What does Lion do?

Write clues that show how Lion is different from the rest of the animals.

What the other animals do	What Lion does

How does the author change the story with Lion?

_____

- -

_____

- -

_____

Check In 1 > 2 > 3 > 4 >

Write About the Anchor Text

Based on the story, what is something Rabbit might be thinking about at the end? Use evidence from the text in your answer.

Talk about the question.

Write your answer below.

_____

- -

_____

- -

_____

- -

_____

- -

_____

- -

_____

Remember:

☐ Use descriptive words.

☐ Focus on one topic.

☐ Use the verbs *was* and *were* correctly.

38 Unit 4 · Week 1

Check In   1   2   3   4

Animals Can Go Fast!

What moves at top speed? A plane? A train? How about a bird, a fish, or even a big cat? Many animals move fast. Mostly they are trying to catch other animals. Or trying not to get caught!

What helps them go fast? Let's look and learn.

Read to find out about how fast some animals can move.

Underline the sentences that tell you why animals move fast.

Talk about why the author chose this photo for the text.

Read the chart. It tells ways animals go fast to stay alive.

Animal	What Helps Them to Go Fast	Speed
Peregrine falcon	Wings, body shape	200 miles an hour
Cheetah	Long thin body, long legs, long tail	70 miles an hour
Sailfish	Foldable fin	68 miles an hour
Brown hare	Long hind legs	45 miles an hour

(t-b)SteveOehlenschlager/iStock/Getty Images; Elliott Neep/Flickr/Getty Images; Kit Korzun/Shutterstock; Mark Medcalf/Shutterstock

Underline the names of animals that have long legs.

Circle the text in the chart that tells how fast a cheetah can go.

Talk about how the chart helps you understand the text better.

Quick Tip

Read the headings in the chart first.

Talk about what you learn about these fast animals from the chart.

 Write clues from the chart.

What helps the peregrine falcon go fast?	
What helps the sailfish go fast?	

How does the author help you learn why each animal can move fast?

_____

- -

_____

- -

_____

Talk About It

How does the author show that these animals' bodies help them?

Check In 1 > 2 > 3 > 4

Animal Bodies

Step 1 **Pick** an animal to research. Find out how its body helps it live, move, or eat.

_____

- -

_____

Step 2 **Decide** what you want to know about the animal. Write your questions.

_____

- -

_____

_____

_____

- -

_____

Step 3 **Decide** where to find the information you need.

Step 4 **Write** what you learned about the animal.

_____

_____

_____

_____

_____

_____

_____

Step 5 **Draw** the animal. Label its body parts.

Step 6 **Choose** how to present your work.

Check In	1	2	3	4

Talk about what the caption tells you about arctic hares.

Compare what these hares and the animals in "Animals Can Go Fast!" do to stay alive. Use complete sentences.

The arctic hare's fur turns white in winter. This makes the hare hard to find in the snow.

Quick Tip

You can compare the animals using these sentence starters:

Arctic hares have . . .

Animals that move fast have . . .

Check In 1 2 3 4

My Goal — I know about ways animals' bodies can help them.

Write a Nonfiction Text

1. **Look** at your Build Knowledge pages in your reader's notebook. What did you learn about how animals' bodies help them?

2. **Write** about an animal and how it uses its body. Then compare it to two other animals you read about. Use text evidence. Use two vocabulary words from the Word Bank.

3. **Draw** a picture to go with your writing.

Think about what you learned this week. Fill in the bars on page 13.

Build Knowledge

Build Vocabulary

 Talk with your partner about ways animals can help each other.

 Write words that tell how they help each other.

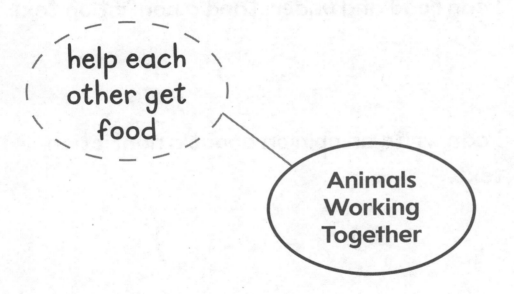

help each other get food

Animals Working Together

My Goals

Think about what you know now. You'll learn a lot more this week. Fill in the bars.

What I Know Now

I can read and understand a nonfiction text.

1 2 3 4

I can write an opinion about a nonfiction text.

1 2 3 4

I know about ways animals help each other.

1 2 3 4

Key

1 =	I do not understand.
2 =	I understand but need more practice.
3 =	I understand.
4 =	I understand and can teach someone.

 STOP You will come back to the next page later.

What I Learned

I can read and understand a nonfiction text.

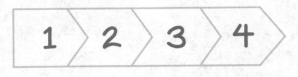

I can write an opinion about a nonfiction text.

1 2 3 4

I know about ways animals help each other.

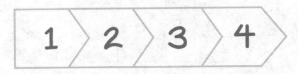

My Goal

I can read and understand a nonfiction text.

🔍 **Find Text Evidence**

 Read the title. Look at the photo. Think about what you want to learn from this text.

Circle and read aloud the word with the long *e* sound spelled *ea*.

A Team of Fish

Find Text Evidence

Underline and read aloud the words *blue, into,* and *or.*

 Ask any questions you may have about the text. Read to find the answer.

Fish swim in lakes and creeks. Fish swim in deep blue seas or oceans.

Let's dive into the water. Let's look at fish!

Georgette Douwma/Stone/Getty Images

Fish can swim alone. Fish can swim with a **partner**.

Fish can swim in a bunch, too. A bunch of fish is called a school.

Shared Read

Reinhard Dirscherl/Alamy Stock Photo

 Find Text Evidence

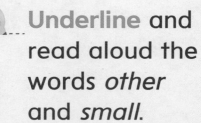 **Talk** about why a school of fish is a team.

Underline and read aloud the words *other* and *small*.

A school has lots of fish. They are a team.

The fish help each other. They look for food together.

Fish eat lots of things. Some fish eat <u>small</u> animals. Some fish eat <u>other</u> fish!

These catfish eat together for safety.

Shared Read

🔍 **Find Text Evidence**

✏ **Circle** and read aloud the word with the long *e* sound spelled *ie*.

Ask any questions you may have about the text. Read to find the answer.

It can be unsafe to swim alone. What is the chief reason? **Danger**! A fish can get snapped up!

But a fish can hide in a school.

Fish in a school have a neat trick. The fish swim close together.

Big fish will not mess with them because they look like one huge fish.

These crescent-tail bigeye fish swim in a school to fool big fish.

Find Text Evidence

Retell the text using the photos and words.

This big fish wants to eat. But it stays away. The school looks like a huge fish that may eat him!

Georgette Douwma/Stone/Getty Images

Fish in a school keep each other safe.

A school is a good place for a fish to be!

Hundreds of barracuda fish swim in a school together.

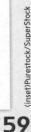

Write Sentences

A Team of Fish

 Talk about how fish work as a team.

 Listen to these sentences about teamwork.

I like to cook with my family. It is fun to mix the ingredients. We all work together!

 Circle the sentence that introduces the topic.

Underline reasons for the opinion.

Writing Traits

- The first sentence often introduces **the topic.**

- Remember, always include **reasons for an opinion** in your writing.

Talk about what it's like to work with a team.

 Write sentences about whether you prefer to work alone or with a team. Give reasons for your opinion. Include a topic sentence.

_____

_____

_____

_____

_____

Circle the sentence that introduces the topic.

Underline reasons for your opinion.

Check In 1 ⟩ 2 ⟩ 3 ⟩ 4 ⟩

Vocabulary

 Listen to the sentences and look at the photos.

 Talk about the words.

 Write your own sentence using each word.

danger

Mom keeps her cub out of **danger**.

_____

- -

_____

partner

A **partner** is a big help.

_____

- -

_____

If you don't know what a word means, look at other words in the sentence for clues.

Find Text Evidence

I'm not sure what *oceans* means. The words *swim in deep blue seas* give me hints about the meaning. I think *oceans* are some kind of water.

Fish swim in lakes and creeks. Fish swim in deep blue seas or oceans.

Your Turn

What words can help you figure out the meaning of *school* on page 53?

_____

_____

_____

_____

_____

_____

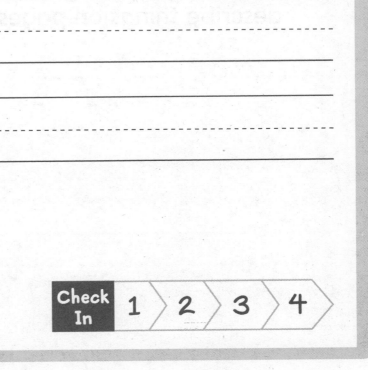

Nonfiction is a genre. A nonfiction text can give facts about real things. It can include words and phrases that describe these things.

 Reread "A Team of Fish."

 Talk about the words and phrases that describe things on page 52.

Write about the words and phrases that describe things on pages 57 and 58.

Word or Phrase	What It Describes

The **topic** is what the text is mostly about.
Relevant details give information about
the topic.

 Reread "A Team of Fish."

 Talk about the topic and relevant details in the text. Use the words and pictures.

Write the topic and relevant details about why fish swim in schools.

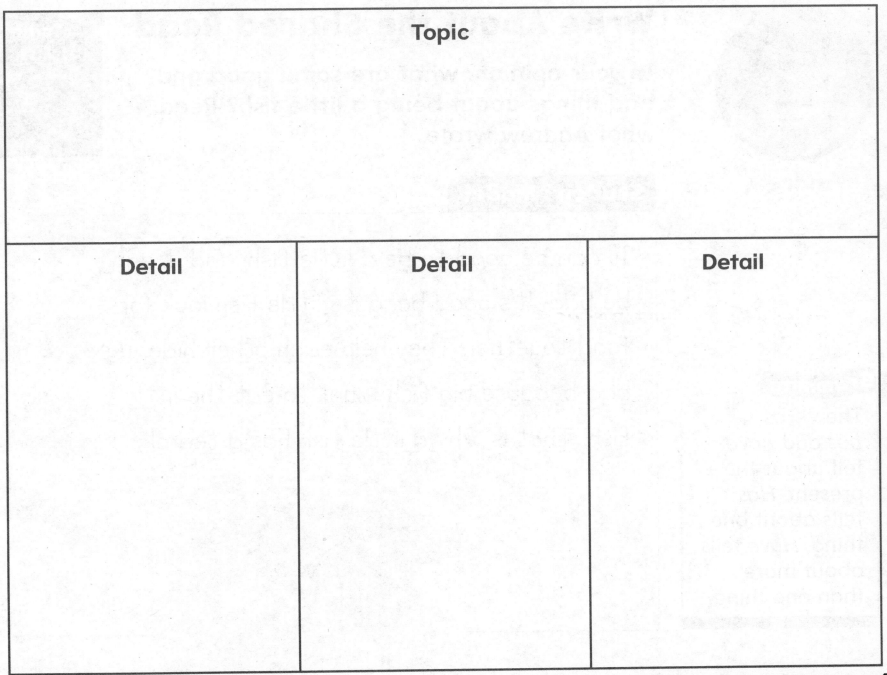

Topic

Detail

Detail

Detail

Andrew

Write About the Shared Read

In your opinion, what are some good and bad things about being a little fish? Read what Andrew wrote.

A Team of Fish

Student Model

It can be good to be a little fish, and it can be bad. It's good because little fish look for food together. They help each other hide. It's bad because big fish want to eat the little fish. That is why a little fish has a team!

Jessica lewis/Moment/Getty Images

Grammar

The verbs *has* and *have* tell about the present. *Has* tells about one thing. *Have* tells about more than one thing.

Talk about details Andrew used from the text. Underline the topic sentence.

 Circle the word *has*.

 Draw a box around each of the reasons for Andrew's opinion.

Write what you notice about Andrew's writing.

Quick Tip

You can talk about Andrew's writing using these sentence starters:

I noticed . . .
Andrew used . . .

Animal Teams
By Rachel Mann

Retell the text in your own words.

Write about the text.

Why does the clown fish live in a sea anemone?

_____

- -

_____

_____

- -

_____

Text Evidence

Page

Why do ants help caterpillars?

_____

- -

_____

_____

- -

_____

Text Evidence

Page

Check In 1 2 3 4

Talk about how the animals on pages 42–43 help each other.

 Write clues from the text and photos to complete the chart.

What the Text Says	What the Photos Show

How do the text and photos help you understand how the animals work as a team?

_____

- -

_____

- -

_____

 Talk about the question the author asks at the end of page 44.

 Write clues from the text that answer the author's question.

Clues

How does the author help you understand the information about this animal team?

_____

- -

_____

- -

_____

Share how the animals on pages 48–51 help each other.

 Write what you learn about animal teams on these pages.

Pages 48–49	Pages 50–51

Why does the author show so many different animal teams?

_____

- -

_____

- -

_____

Write About the Anchor Text

Which animal team do you think is most interesting? Why?

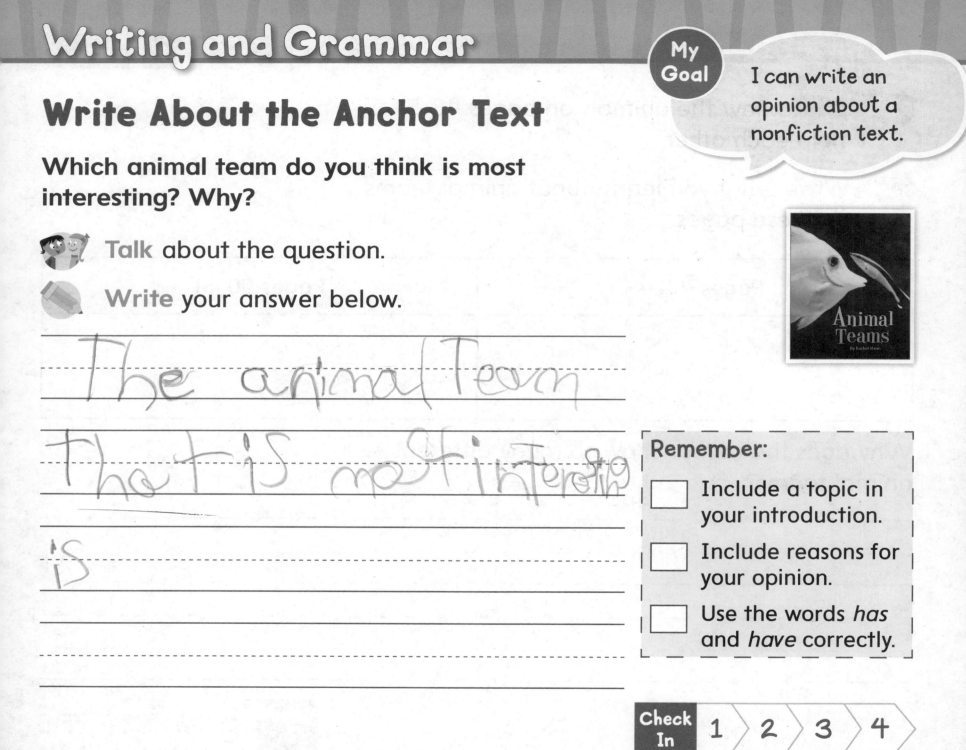

Talk about the question.

Write your answer below.

The animal Team That is most interesting is

Remember:

☐ Include a topic in your introduction.

☐ Include reasons for your opinion.

☐ Use the words *has* and *have* correctly.

Check In 1 2 3 4

Busy as a Bee

Lots of worker bees help make honey. They help keep the hive clean, too.

Worker bees make wax cups called honeycombs.

Read to find out how bees work together as a team.

Circle the word that tells what wax cups are called.

Talk about how the author shows that bees are busy.

(t)Jan Rietz/Nordic Photos/Getty Images; (b)Ted Horowitz/Corbis/Getty Images

Every hive has a queen bee. She lays all the eggs.

A hive has drone bees, too. A drone's job is to help the queen make eggs.

A queen bee is with her drones in the hive.

 Underline the sentence that tells what a queen bee does.

Circle the text that tells who else lives in the hive.

Talk about the photo and the caption. Why does the author include both?

Quick Tip

Think about what the photo and caption tell you about bees.

Talk about the title of the text.

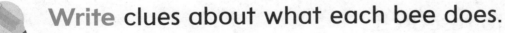 **Write** clues about what each bee does.

Worker Bees	Queen Bee	Drone Bees

How does the title help you understand the topic of the text?

_____

- -

_____

- -

_____

Talk About It

How does the author show that every bee in a hive has a special job?

Check In 1 ⟩ 2 ⟩ 3 ⟩ 4 ⟩

Animal Teams

Step 1 **Pick** a team of animals to research.

_____

- -

_____

Step 2 **Decide** where to find the information you need.

_____

- -

_____

Step 3 **Draw** the animal team you learned about.
Use labels to name each animal.

Step 4 **Write** what you learned about the animal team.

_____

- -

_____

_____

- -

_____

_____

- -

_____

_____

- -

_____

Step 5 **Choose** how to present your work.

Check In   1   2   3   4

Talk about how the birds in the photo are a team.

 Compare how these birds are similar to the school of fish you read about.

It is safe to be in a big group. These birds flock together to stay safe.

Quick Tip

You can talk about this photo using these sentence starters:

Birds fly together to . . .

The birds help one another . . .

Check In   1 > 2 > 3 > 4

Create a Teamwork Trophy

1 **Look** at your Build Knowledge pages in your reader's notebook. What did you learn about how animals help each other?

2 **Think** about which animals should get a teamwork trophy. Write why this team has earned the award. Then compare these animals to other animals you read about. Use evidence to support your opinion. Use two vocabulary words from the Word Bank.

3 **Draw or create** a Teamwork Trophy.

Think about what you learned this week. Fill in the bars on page 49.

Build Knowledge

Essential Question How do animals survive in nature?

Build Vocabulary

 Talk with your partner about ways animals survive in nature.

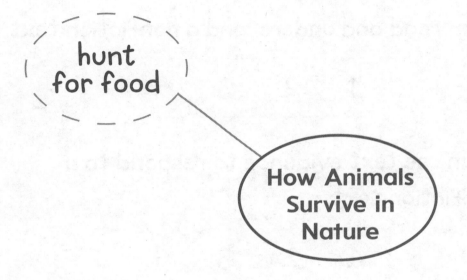 **Write** words about animals in nature.

hunt for food

How Animals Survive in Nature

My Goals

Think about what you know now. It will be fun to learn more. Fill in the bars.

What I Know Now

I can read and understand a nonfiction text.

1 > 2 > 3 > 4

I can use text evidence to respond to a nonfiction text.

1 > 2 > 3 > 4

I know about ways animals survive in nature.

1 > 2 > 3 > 4

Key

1 = I do not understand.

2 = I understand but need more practice.

3 = I understand.

4 = I understand and can teach someone.

 You will come back to the next page later.

Think about what you've learned.
Keep trying. Fill in the bars.

What I Learned

I can read and understand a nonfiction text.

1 2 3 4

I can use text evidence to respond to a nonfiction text.

1 2 3 4

I know about ways animals survive in nature.

1 2 3 4

Shared Read

? How do animals survive in nature?

My Goal I can read and understand a nonfiction text.

 Find Text Evidence

 Read to find out how animals survive in the wild.

Circle and read aloud the word with the same ending sound as *toe*.

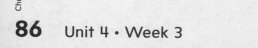

GO WILD!

Find Text Evidence

 Underline and read aloud the words *food*, *more*, and *find*.

Ask yourself any questions you may have about the text. Read to find the answer.

Animals need food to live and grow. But all animals don't eat the same things. Some big animals such as hippos eat plants. A hippo can eat more than 130 pounds of grass!

Some small animals eat plants, too. A squirrel eats loads of plant seeds. They like nuts and grains. A squirrel can smell a nut and find it even in the snow!

Alex Fieldhouse/Alamy Stock Photo

Shared Read

Andy Rouse/The Image Bank/Getty Images

 Find Text Evidence

 Talk about the big cat. How does it hunt?

Circle and read aloud the words with the long *o* sound spelled *oa*.

Some animals hunt and eat other animals. First this big cat runs fast to catch its meal. Then it will use its claws and teeth to eat.

Frogs and toads **seek** insects and snails to eat. A big frog goes after mice, too. But frogs and toads have no teeth. So they must gulp down their meal!

Ask yourself any questions you may have about the text. Read to find the answer.

Underline and read aloud the words *over* and *warm*.

Some animals eat both plants and animals. An ostrich eats seeds and leaves. But it will **search** all over for insects, snakes, and lizards as well.

Carl & Ann Purcell/Corbis Documentary/Getty Images

A painted turtle eats plants, fish, and frogs. This reptile lives in lakes and ponds. It likes the cold water at first. But then it will come up on land to get warm.

Find Text Evidence

 Talk about how much the different animals eat in a day.

Retell the text using the photos and words.

A bear may start its day at a lake. It can use its strong sense of smell to find fish. Next, a bear may look in the woods.

A bear can use long claws to dig. It may find fruit and plants to eat.

In the wild, animals find food in lots of places.

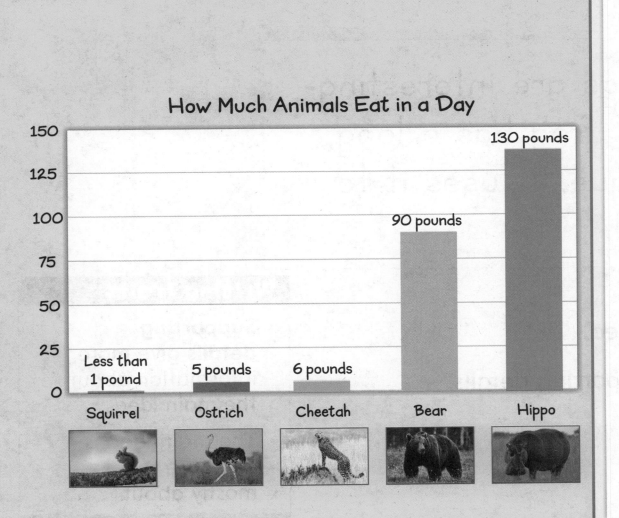

How Much Animals Eat in a Day

Squirrel — Less than 1 pound
Ostrich — 5 pounds
Cheetah — 6 pounds
Bear — 90 pounds
Hippo — 130 pounds

Write Sentences

 Talk about animals in the wild.

 Listen to these sentences about an animal in the wild.

I think frogs are interesting animals. A frog has a long, sticky tongue. It uses it to grab bugs!

 **Circle** the main idea.

Underline the supporting details.

Writing Traits

- **Supporting details** give more information about the main idea.

- The **main idea** is what the text is mostly about.

Talk about your favorite wild animal.

Write sentences about your favorite wild animal. Make sure you include a main idea and supporting details.

_____

- -

_____

- -

_____

- -

_____

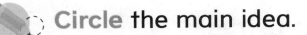 **Circle** the main idea.

Underline the supporting details.

Vocabulary

 Listen to the sentences and look at the photos.

 Talk about the words.

Write your own sentence using each word.

search

Do bees **search** for plants?

_____

- - - - - - - - - - - - - - - - - - -

_____

seek

A bear will **seek** out ripe berries.

_____

- - - - - - - - - - - - - - - - - - -

_____

Word Categories

As we read, we can look for groups of words that are alike in some ways.

🔍 Find Text Evidence

I can find words that fit in the same category. The words *seeds, nuts,* and *grains* name things that squirrels eat. I will look for other words that fit in the category of *things that animals eat.*

> Frogs and toads seek (insects) and (snails) to eat. A big frog goes after (mice) too.

Your Turn

What words belong in the category *animal names* on page 92?

_____

_____

_____

_____

Check In 1 ⟩ 2 ⟩ 3 ⟩ 4 ⟩

Nonfiction is a genre. A nonfiction text can give facts about real things. It can explain how something happens.

 Reread "Go Wild!"

 Share what squirrels eat. How does the author describe how they find food?

Write about how other animals find food.

Check In | 1 2 3 4

Animal	How It Finds Food
I.	I.
2.	2.
3.	3.

Remember, the **topic** is what the text is mostly about. **Relevant details** give information about the topic.

 Reread "Go Wild!"

 **Talk** about the topic of the text.

Write about the topic and relevant details from the text.

Check In 1 2 3 4

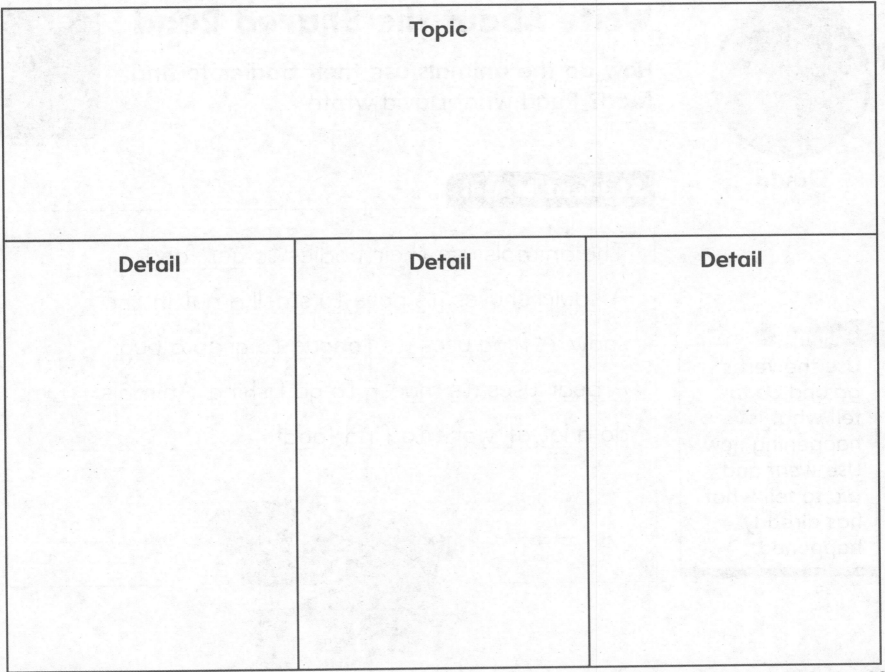

Topic		
Detail	**Detail**	**Detail**

David

Write About the Shared Read

How do the animals use their bodies to find food? Read what David wrote.

Grammar

Use the verbs *go* and *do* to tell what is happening now. Use *went* and *did* to tell what has already happened.

Student Model

The animals use their bodies to get food.
A squirrel uses its nose to smell a nut in the
snow. A frog uses its tongue to grab a bug.
A bear uses its mouth to go fishing. Animals
do a lot of work to find food!

Talk about details David used from the text. Underline the supporting details.

 Circle the words *go* and *do*.

 Draw a box around the main idea.

 Write what you notice about David's writing.

Respond to the **Anchor Text**

 Retell the text in your own words.

Write about the text.

What type of food do the turkey vultures look for?

Text Evidence

Pages

What do the turkey vultures do after they eat?

Text Evidence

Page

Check In 1 2 3 4

Talk about what the vultures are doing on pages 64–67.

 Write clues from the text to complete the chart. Use the illustrations to help you.

What does the text describe?	
What do the illustrations show?	

How does the author help you picture what is happening?

_____

_____

_____

_____

_____

Talk about the illustrations on pages 76–79.

Write clues from the illustrations that help you understand what the vultures are doing.

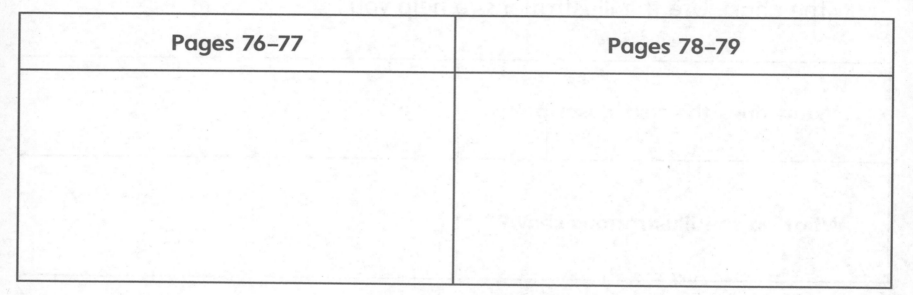

Pages 76–77	Pages 78–79

How do the illustrations help you understand how vultures eat?

_____

- -

_____

- -

_____

Talk about how the author describes the vultures' wings on pages 82 and 86.

Write the words on the chart.

Page 82	Page 86

What do the author's words help you picture? Share your answer.

_____

_____

_____

_____

My Goal I can use text evidence to respond to a nonfiction text.

Write About the Anchor Text

How do vultures use their body parts to help them find food?

 Talk about the question.

 Write your answer below.

_____

- - - - - - - - - - - - - - - - - - -

_____

- - - - - - - - - - - - - - - - - - -

_____

- - - - - - - - - - - - - - - - - - -

_____

- - - - - - - - - - - - - - - - - - -

_____

Remember:

☐ Use supporting details.

☐ Include a main idea.

☐ Use *go* and *do* correctly.

Check In 1 > 2 > 3 > 4

"When It's Snowing"

 Talk about the illustration on pages 90–91.

 **Write** clues that show how it feels outside and inside the mouse's house.

Outside	Inside

How does the illustration help you understand the poem's setting?

_____

- -

_____

- -

_____

Talk about the beat you hear in the poem.
Clap the rhythm you hear in lines 1 and 2.

Write the number of beats that you hear.

Number of beats in lines 1 and 2	
Number of beats in lines 3 and 4	

How does the rhythm of the poem make you feel?

_____

- - - - - - - - - - - - - - - - - - -

_____

- - - - - - - - - - - - - - - - - - -

_____

Quick Tip

You can clap your hands as you read a poem to find the beat.

Talk about the question in the first paragraph.

Write clues that help you know how the poet feels about the mouse.

How poet refers to the mouse	What poet asks the mouse

How do you know the poet cares about the mouse?

_____

- -

_____

- -

_____

Check In 1 2 3 4

Animal Life Cycle

Step 1 **Pick** an animal to research.
Find out about its life cycle.

_____

- -

_____

Step 2 **Decide** what you want to know about
the animal. Write your questions.

_____

- -

_____

_____

- -

_____

_____

- -

_____

Step 3 **Use** books from the library to find information.

Step 4 Write what you learned about the animal.

_____
- - - - - - - - - - - - - - - - -
_____
- - - - - - - - - - - - - - - - -
_____
- - - - - - - - - - - - - - - - -
_____
- - - - - - - - - - - - - - - - -
_____
- - - - - - - - - - - - - - - - -
_____
- - - - - - - - - - - - - - - - -
_____
- - - - - - - - - - - - - - - - -

Step 5 Draw the animal.

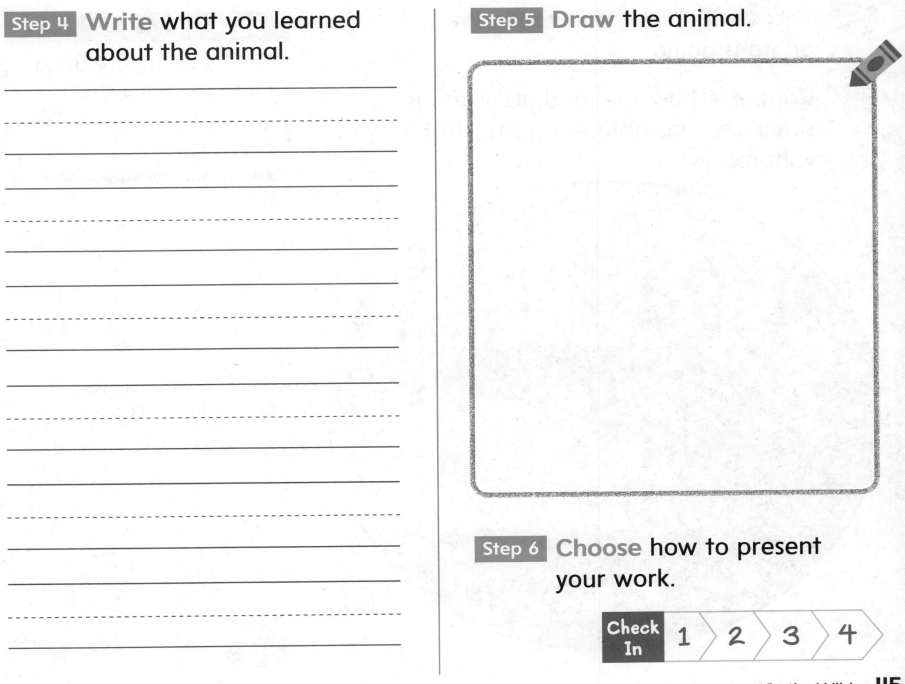

Step 6 Choose how to present your work.

Check In 1 > 2 > 3 > 4 >

Make Connections

 Talk about what the orca in the photo is doing.

 Compare how the food orcas eat is similar to and different from what vultures eat.

Quick Tip

You can compare using these sentence starters:

Vultures eat . . .
Orcas eat . . .

Orcas eat live fish and animals. They hunt for food in the sea.

Check In 1 2 3 4

Write a Science Article

1 **Look** at your Build Knowledge pages in your reader's notebook. What did you learn about how animals survive in nature?

2 **Write** a science article. Tell how three of the animals you learned about survive in nature. Use text evidence. Use two vocabulary words from the Word Bank.

3 **Create** a diagram with labels for your article.

Think about what you learned this week. Fill in the bars on page 85.

Build Knowledge

Essential Question What insects do you know? How are they alike and different?

Build Vocabulary

 Talk with your partner about insects you know.

 Write words about insects.

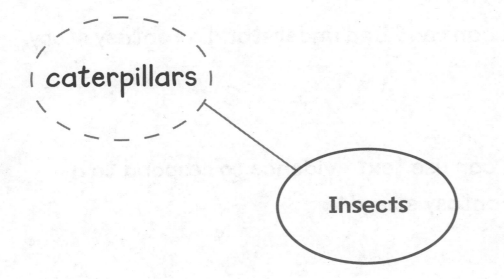

caterpillars

Insects

My Goals

Think about what you know now. It's important to do your best. Fill in the bars.

What I Know Now

I can read and understand a fantasy story.

I can use text evidence to respond to a fantasy story.

I know about insects and how they are alike and different.

Key

1 = I do not understand.

2 = I understand but need more practice.

3 = I understand.

4 = I understand and can teach someone.

 You will come back to the next page later.

Think about what you've learned. What helped you the most? Fill in the bars.

What I Learned

I can read and understand a fantasy story.

1　2　3　4

I can use text evidence to respond to a fantasy story.

1　2　3　4

I know about insects and how they are alike and different.

1　2　3　4

Shared Read

My Goal

I can read and understand a fantasy story.

 Find Text Evidence

 Read to find out about what some insects are like.

Circle and read aloud the word with the long *i* sound spelled *-y*.

Gregor Schuster/SuperStock

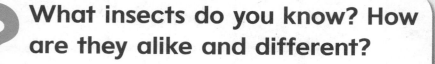

Essential Question

? What insects do you know? How are they alike and different?

Creep Low, Fly High

Shared Read

 Find Text Evidence

 Underline and read aloud the words *laugh* and *listen*.

Think about the words *zip around*. How do they help you picture how Ladybug moves?

Bug Boasts

The Sun came up over a big field. Five bug pals met to chat and laugh.

Grasshopper boasted a bit. "I can hop to the top of any plant!"

"Well, I can dash fast," bragged Ant.

"Listen!" hummed Bee. "I can buzz as I fly high."

"And I can zip around on **fancy** spotted wings!" smiled Ladybug.

🔍 **Find Text Evidence**

Think about how Caterpillar feels. Why does he sigh and creep away?

Circle and read aloud the word with the long *i* sound spelled *-igh*.

"Not I," sighed Caterpillar. "I just creep, creep, creep." Then he crept away.

"Come back!" his pals wailed. But Caterpillar did not.

Missing!

It was time for lunch. The bugs did not see Caterpillar. He was missing! Where did he go?

Shared Read

🔍 **Find Text Evidence**

 Talk about what Bee says. Picture the bird in your mind. What do you think it was doing?

Underline the words *know*, *where*, *flew*, and *caught*.

"I think I know where he is!" cried Ant. "He is hiding because he feels bad."

"I think that's right," nodded Grasshopper. "Let's find him. We can cheer him up!"

The two rushed away.

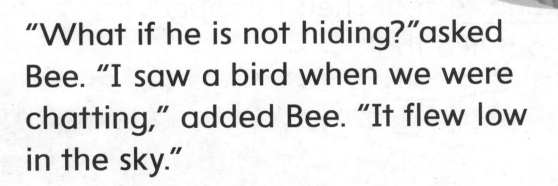

"What if he is not hiding?"asked Bee. "I saw a bird when we were chatting," added Bee. "It flew low in the sky."

"What if it caught our pal?" cried Ladybug. "We must find out! Maybe we can save him!"

The two flew away.

🔍 **Find Text Evidence**

Retell the story using the illustrations and words.

Still a Pal

The bugs did not find Caterpillar. Many days went by. The pals were sad. Then one day they saw a **beautiful** bug with gold wings.

"Hi! I'm back!" the bug called as he flew by. "I wrapped up and rested. Then I popped out like this!"

"It's me—Butterfly! I used to be Caterpillar!" cried Butterfly.

"But you are not the same," sighed Ant.

"But I am still a pal," said Butterfly. "And now I can flit and dip! Let's go have some fun!"

Write Sentences

 Talk about the insects in the story.

Listen to these sentences about insects.

Creep Low, Fly High

> My favorite insect is a caterpillar. They have many legs. They grow up to be beautiful butterflies.

 **Circle** the descriptive details.

Underline the concluding statement.

Writing Traits

- Remember, **descriptive details** can make writing more interesting.

- A **concluding statement** tells the ending of a story or text.

Talk about your favorite insect.

 Write sentences about your favorite insect. Make sure you include descriptive details and a concluding statement.

_____

_____

_____

_____

 Circle the descriptive details you used.

 Underline the concluding statement.

Vocabulary

 Listen to the sentences and look at the photos.

 Talk about the words.

 Write your own sentence using each word.

beautiful

The butterfly has **beautiful** wings.

_____

- -

_____

fancy

We are wearing **fancy** hats.

_____

- -

_____

Context Clues

When you are not sure of what a word means, you can look at how it is used in the sentence.

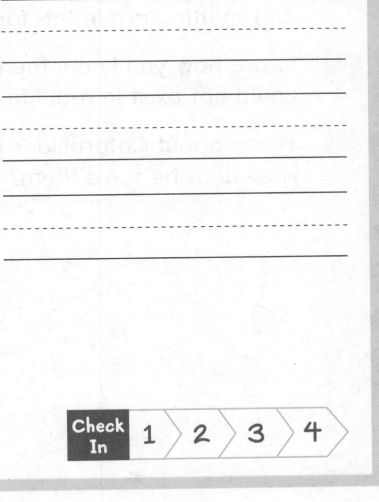

Find Text Evidence

I'm not sure what *chat* means. The word *laugh* is a hint. I know that the bugs are pals so they must have been talking together. I think *chat* means *to talk in a friendly way*.

Five bug pals met to (chat) and (laugh.)

Your Turn

What is the meaning of *dash* on page 125 of the story?

_____

- - - - - - - - - - - - - - - - - - -

_____

- - - - - - - - - - - - - - - - - - -

_____

_____

- - - - - - - - - - - - - - - - - - -

_____

Check In 1 > 2 > 3 > 4 >

A **fantasy** story can have characters that could not exist in real life. It often has a problem and solution.

Creep Low, Fly High

 Reread to find out what the problem and solution are in this fantasy story.

 Share how you know the characters could not exist in real life.

Write about Caterpillar's problems. How does he solve them?

Check In 1 2 3 4

What is the problem?	What is the solution?
1.	1.
2.	2.
3.	3.

A **narrator** is who tells the story.

I. The narrator can be a character in the story. This narrator uses the words *I, me*, and *my*.

2. The narrator can be a speaker outside the story. This narrator uses characters' names and words like *he, his*, and *they*.

 Reread "Creep Low, Fly High."

 Talk about who is telling the story. Look for clues on pages I26 and I30.

 Write the clues. Then write who is telling the story.

Check In 1 2 3 4

Clues on page 126	Clues on page 130

Who Is Telling the Story?

Writing and Grammar

Amy

Write About the Shared Read

Creep Low, Fly High

How do Caterpillar's feelings change from the beginning to the end of the story? Read what Amy wrote.

Grammar

Use *see* when looking at something now. Use *sees* when he or she is looking now. Use *saw* to tell about looking in the past.

Student Model

In the beginning, Caterpillar is sad. He can't dash fast or fly high. Then his friends see he changes into a beautiful butterfly. At the end of the story, he is very happy. Now he can flit and dip!

Talk about details Amy used from the story. Underline the concluding statement.

 Circle the word *see*.

 Draw boxes around the descriptive details in the second sentence.

 Write what you notice about Amy's writing.

Quick Tip

You can talk about Amy's writing using these sentence starters:

Amy used . . .
I noticed . . .

Retell the story in your own words.

Write about the story.

How does the boy catch the fly?

_____

_____

_____

Text Evidence

Page

What convinces the judges that
Fly Guy is a pet?

_____

_____

_____

Text Evidence

Page

Check In | 1 | 2 | 3 | 4

Talk about how the fly and the boy are feeling on pages 102–103.

 Write clues from the pictures and text that show you how the characters are feeling.

How the Fly Feels	How the Boy Feels

How does the author show you how the fly and the boy feel?

_____

- -

_____

- -

_____

Anchor Text

Talk about the events on pages 112–115. How do the judges' faces change?

Write clues from the illustrations that help you understand how the judges feel.

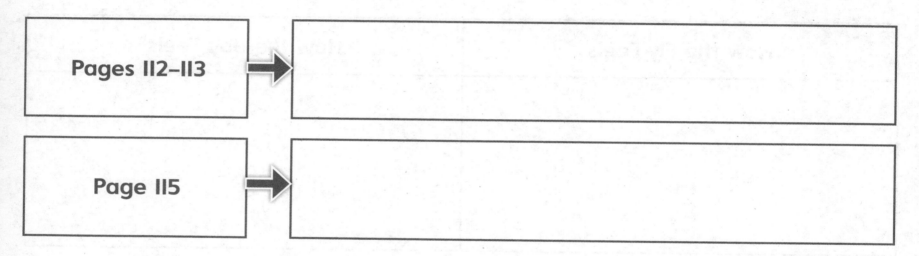

| Pages 112–113 → | |
| Page 115 → | |

How do the illustrations help you know the judges' point of view?

_____

- -

_____

- -

_____

Talk about pages 117–121. How does Fly Guy show the judges that he is a pet?

Write clues from the text and illustrations.

What Fly Guy Does	What the Judges Do

How does the author show that Fly Guy can be a pet?

_____

- -

_____

- -

_____

Check In 1 2 3 4

Write About the Anchor Text

Why do Buzz's parents and the judges change their minds about Fly Guy?

 Talk about the question.

 Write your answer below.

_____

- - - - - - - - - - - - - - - - - - - -

_____

- - - - - - - - - - - - - - - - - - - -

_____

- - - - - - - - - - - - - - - - - - - -

_____

- - - - - - - - - - - - - - - - - - - -

_____

- - - - - - - - - - - - - - - - - - - -

_____

Remember:

☐ Include a concluding statement.

☐ Add descriptive details.

☐ Use *see* and *saw* correctly.

Check In 1 > 2 > 3 > 4 >

Meet the Insects

The Body of an Insect

All insects have six legs and three body parts. Insects have no bones. The outside of an insect's body is hard. It protects the insect's body. Most insects have antennae and wings.

 Read to find out what insects can do.

Underline the text that tells you what most insects have.

Talk about the heading. How does the heading help you understand the text on this page?

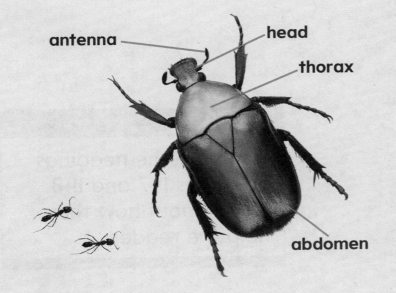

antenna — head

thorax

abdomen

Insect Senses

Insects use their senses to find food. A fly smells with its antennae.
It tastes with its feet. That's why flies like to land on food.

Insects do not see the same as we do. Many insects have more than two eyes. A grasshopper has five!

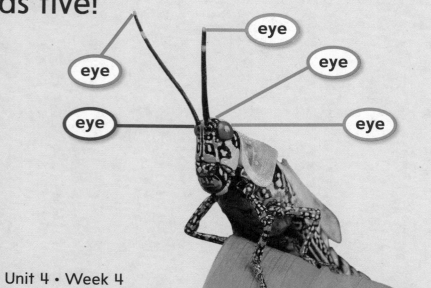

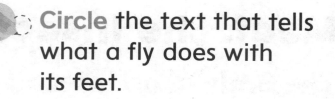 **Circle** the text that tells what a fly does with its feet.

Underline the sentence that tells how many eyes a grasshopper has.

 Talk about why the author uses headings in the text.

Quick Tip

Compare the headings on pages 147 and 148. Think about how they help the reader.

Simon Murrell/Cultura/Getty Images

Talk about what the photos help you understand about insects.

 Write clues from the photos to complete the chart.

What information does the photo on page 147 provide?	
What information does the photo on page 148 provide?	

How do the labels help you understand what insects are like?

_____

- -

_____

_____

- -

_____

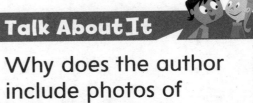

Talk About It

Why does the author include photos of different insects?

Compare Two Insects

Step 1 **Pick** two insects you read about to compare their body parts.

_____

_____

Step 2 **Use** books from the library or the Internet to find the information you need.

Step 3 **Draw** the insects below.

Step 4 Write about how the insects are alike and different.

_____

- -

_____

- -

_____

- -

_____

- -

_____

- -

_____

- -

_____

Step 5 Choose how to present your work.

Check In 1 > 2 > 3 > 4

Talk about what the photo shows you about dragonflies.

 Compare how the body parts of this dragonfly are alike or different from insects in "Creep Low, Fly High."

Quick Tip

You can describe dragonflies using these sentence starters:

Dragonflies have . . .

Dragonflies are insects because . . .

A dragonfly has three body parts. This dragonfly has a blue head and abdomen. Its thorax is green with black stripes.

ChatchawalPhumkaew/iStock/Getty Images

Check In 1 2 3 4

152 Unit 4 • Week 4

Create an Insect Diagram

1 **Look** at your Build Knowledge pages in your reader's notebook. What did you learn about insects and how they are alike and different?

2 **Choose** an insect. Write about how it is alike or different from other insects you read about. Use text evidence. Use two vocabulary words from the Word Bank.

3 **Draw** and label a diagram of your insect.

Think about what you learned this week. Fill in the bars on page 121.

Build Knowledge

Essential Question **How do people work with animals?**

Build Vocabulary

 Talk with your partner about ways people work with animals.

Write words about working with animals.

(rescue)

How People Work with Animals

My Goals

Think about what you know now. Everyone learns more with practice. Fill in the bars.

What I Know Now

I can read and understand a nonfiction text.

I can use text evidence to respond to a nonfiction text.

1 2 3 4

I know about ways people work with animals.

Key

1 = I do not understand.

2 = I understand but need more practice.

3 = I understand.

4 = I understand and can teach someone.

STOP You will come back to the next page later.

Think about what you've learned.
What helped you do your best?
Fill in the bars.

What I Learned

I can read and understand a nonfiction text.

1 > 2 > 3 > 4

I can use text evidence to respond to a nonfiction text.

1 > 2 > 3 > 4

I know about ways people work with animals.

1 > 2 > 3 > 4

My Goal
I can read and understand a nonfiction text.

🔍 **Find Text Evidence**

Read to find out how people train guide dogs.

Circle and read aloud the word with the long *e* sound spelled *-y.*

From Puppy to Guide Dog

Most dogs are pets. But some dogs help people. What is the key to making a dog a good helping dog?

Find Text Evidence

Underline and read aloud the word *found*.

Picture in your mind a lazy or fussy dog. Why do you think it could not be a good guide dog?

A Buddy-to-Be

Mickey is a cute and **clever** puppy. He runs, jumps, and plays. One day, when he grows up a bit, Mickey will be a helping dog. He will be a daily buddy to a person who cannot see.

Helping dogs are called guide dogs. To be a guide dog, a puppy must be bright. It cannot be lazy or fussy. The puppy will need to learn many skills. A new home is found for the puppy when it is eight weeks old.

▼ Guide dogs can be big or tiny.

Fact

Most guide dogs are Labrador retrievers. They are very intelligent and easy to train.

Ryan McVay/Stockbyte/Getty Images

Talk about how a family can help train a puppy. What can they do?

Circle and read aloud the word with the long *e* sound spelled *-ey*.

A Family of Trainers

A puppy like Mickey stays with a family for at least one year. The family plays with it and feeds it. They help the puppy stay healthy and teach the puppy a lot.

▲ Each puppy has checkups at the vet.

Fact

10,000 people in the U.S. and Canada use guide dogs.

Each puppy learns how to act nicely with people and with other animals. The family gets the dog used to a lot of tasks and settings. Puppies may visit many kinds of places in the city. They go to homes and shops.

▲ **This dog watches its favorite team.**

▼ **Every dog must be trained by itself.**

(t)Tom & Dee Ann McCarthy/Corbis/Getty Images; (b)PA/Topham/The Image Works

Picture a dog that stays right near its trainer. Why do you think it is important for the dog to do this?

Underline and read aloud the words *near, woman,* and *hard*.

Learning New Tasks

As time goes by, the dogs are trained how to go across the street. The dog stays right near the trainer. It learns to stop at a red **signal**. This will help the dog safely lead a person who cannot see the traffic.

Fact

Guide dogs are allowed in restaurants, stores, school—any place a person can go.

◄ This guide dog learns to cross a street.

Xinhua/Zumapress.com

Some guide dogs can be trained to help a man or a woman who cannot move or walk. He or she might need help with a lot of hard tasks both inside and outside the home.

A dog can be trained to get an elevator and to reach objects.

Shared Read

Retell the text using the photos and words from the text.

Eyes and Ears

Some dogs are trained to help people who cannot hear. If the dog hears a bell ringing or a yell, it would lightly tug or poke the person with its nose.

▼ A dog can be taught to alert its owner to sounds.

Fact

Guide dogs should not be bothered while working.

Yan Sheng/CNImaging/Newscom

Ready to Guide

Training a puppy for a year is not an easy job. Owners may call or write to thank the family that raised their puppy.

Training a guide dog helps a lot of people!

Juice Images/Alamy Stock Photo

Write Sentences

Talk about what guide dogs can learn to do.

Listen to these sentences about working with animals.

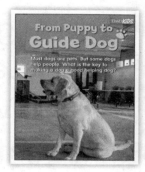

From Puppy to Guide Dog

Most dogs are pets. But some dogs help people. What is the key to making a dog a good helping dog?

> My dad and I walk our dog every morning. We keep him on a leash. He stays very close to us as we walk. He's a good dog!

Underline the topic.

Circle the specific words that tell where the dog stays as they walk.

Writing Traits

- The first sentence can **introduce the topic**.

- Remember, **specific words** are words that say exactly what you mean.

Talk about a time you saw an animal.

 **Write** sentences about a time you saw an animal. Make sure you introduce the topic. Use specific words to make your writing clearer.

Underline the topic.

Circle any specific words you used.

Vocabulary

 Listen to the sentences and look at the photos.

 Talk about the words.

 **Write** your own sentence using each word.

clever

This bird is very **clever**.

_____

- - - - - - - - - - - - - - - - - - - -

_____

signal

The trainer gives a **signal**.

_____

- - - - - - - - - - - - - - - - - - - -

_____

If you don't know what a word means, you can look at its base word to figure out the meaning.

Find Text Evidence

I'm not sure what *helping* means. The word *help* is a hint. I know it means "to give or do something needed or useful." I can figure out that *helping* means "doing something needed or useful."

Mickey will be a helping dog.

Your Turn

What is the meaning of the word *training* on page 167?

_____

_____

_____

_____

Check In 1 2 3 4

A **nonfiction** text can tell facts about real things. It can explain how something happens. It can use photos to give information. Captions give more information about photos.

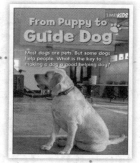

 Reread to find out how this text uses photos and captions.

 Share what you learn from the photo and the caption under the photo on page 162.

 Write what you learn from the photos and captions on pages 164 and 166. Then write what this nonfiction text explains.

Check In   1   2   3   4

The photo and caption on page 164 tell me

The photo and caption on page 166 tell me

What does this nonfiction text explain?

Authors sometimes use **time order** when writing nonfiction. Words such as *first, next, then,* and *last* can help you understand the time order. **Details** in a text can give you information about the time order of events.

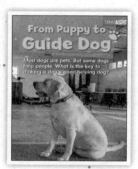

 Reread "From Puppy to Guide Dog."

 Talk about the order of what happens to a guide dog puppy.

 Write the order of steps needed to train a guide dog puppy.

Check In | 1 | 2 | 3 | 4

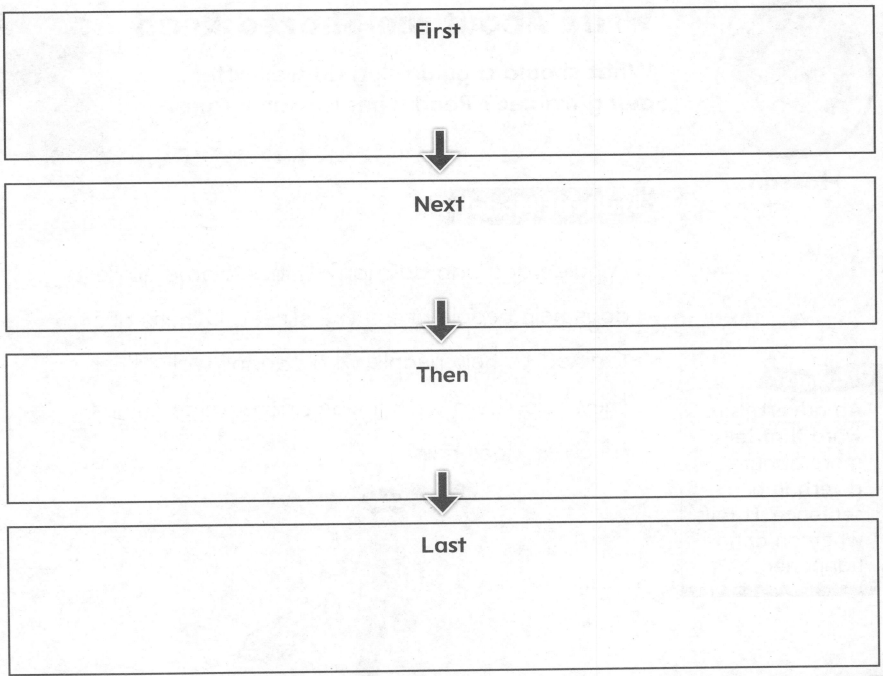

First

Next

Then

Last

Hassan

Write About the Shared Read

What should a guide dog do well after being trained? Read what Hassan wrote.

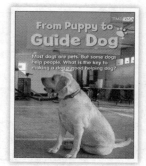

From Puppy to Guide Dog

Most dogs are pets. But some dogs help people. What is the key to making a dog a good helping dog?

Student Model

A guide dog can do many things. Some guide dogs help people cross the street. Others are trained to help people who cannot walk. Then, they help them with inside and outside things. All guide dogs help!

Grammar

An **adverb** is a word that tells more about a verb in a sentence. It tells when an action happened.

Talk about details Hassan used from the text. Underline the topic.

 Circle the adverb that tells when.

 Draw a box around the specific words that tell where dogs help people.

 Write what you notice about Hassan's writing.

Quick Tip

You can talk about Hassan's writing using these sentence starters:

Hassan used . . .
I noticed . . .

_____

_____

_____

_____

_____

_____

 Retell the text in your own words.

Write about the text.

What did Koko ask for the most when she first learned to sign?

_____

- -

_____

- -

_____

Text Evidence

Page

What did Penny do after Koko signed the word "cat" a lot?

_____

- -

_____

_____

- -

_____

Text Evidence

Page

Check In 1 ⟩ 2 ⟩ 3 ⟩ 4 ⟩

Talk about the first thing Penny taught Koko.

Write clues from the text to complete the chart.

What did Penny teach Koko first?	What did Penny teach Koko next?

Why does the author present information in order?

_____

_____

_____

 Talk about the signs Koko makes on pages 132–133.

Write what the captions tell you.

Page 132	Page 133

How do the captions help you understand the photos?

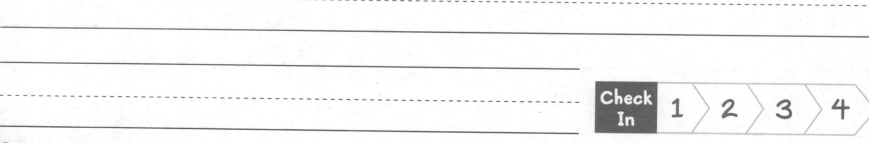

Check In 1 2 3 4

Writing and Grammar

My Goal I can use text evidence to respond to a nonfiction text.

Write About the Anchor Text

How did learning sign language affect Koko's relationship with Penny?

🧑‍🤝‍🧑 **Talk** about the question.

✏️ **Write** your answer below.

_____

_____

_____

_____

_____

_____

_____

_____

Remember:

☐ Introduce your topic.

☐ Use specific words.

☐ Use adverbs that tell when correctly.

Check In 1 2 3 4

Save Our Bees!

Bees need our help!
Many bees are dying.
Scientists think that bugs
or diseases are hurting bees.
Bees are important to us.

Beekeepers work with bees.

Read to find out how you can help save bees.

Circle the word in the caption that tells who works with bees.

Talk about why the author included exclamation marks. What does this tell you?

Monty Rakusen/cultura/Corbis

You can help bees by planting flowers. Bees eat nectar from flowers. Together we can help save bees!

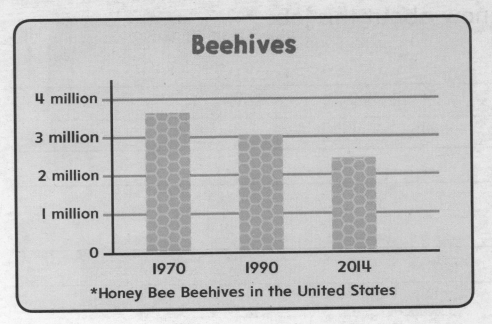

Beehives

4 million
3 million
2 million
1 million
0

1970   1990   2014

*Honey Bee Beehives in the United States

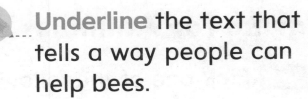 **Underline** the text that tells a way people can help bees.

 Circle the word that tells what bees eat.

Talk about what the author is able to explain by including the graph.

Talk About It

How does the author show that bees can still be saved?

Check In 1 2 3 4

Research and Inquiry

Caring for Animals

Step 1 **Pick** one of the following two jobs to research:

veterinarian   zookeeper

Step 2 **Decide** what you want to know about this job. Write your questions.

_____

_____

_____

_____

_____

_____

Step 3 **Use** books from the library or internet to find the information you need.

Step 4 Write what you learned about the job you researched.

_____

- - - - - - - - - - - - -

_____

- - - - - - - - - - - - -

_____

- - - - - - - - - - - - -

_____

- - - - - - - - - - - - -

_____

- - - - - - - - - - - - -

_____

- - - - - - - - - - - - -

_____

- - - - - - - - - - - - -

_____

Step 5 Draw something you learned.

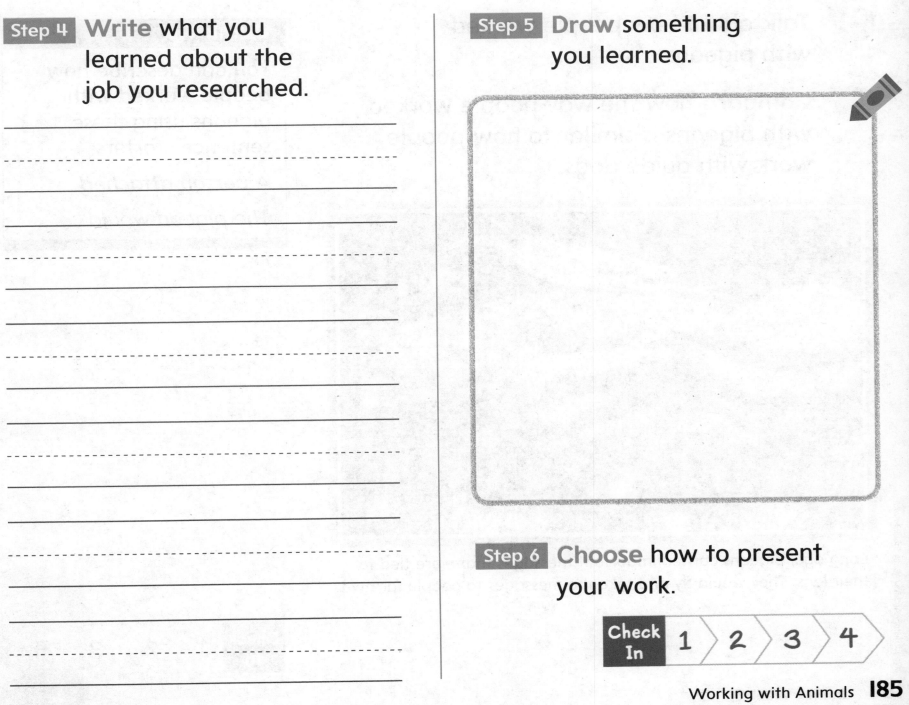

Step 6 Choose how to present your work.

Check In 1 2 3 4

Talk about how people worked with pigeons.

 Compare how the way people worked with pigeons is similar to how people work with guide dogs.

Quick Tip

You can describe how people worked with pigeons using these sentence starters:

A person attached . . .

The pigeon would . . .

Long ago, pigeons carried important messages that were tied to their legs. They would fly and take the messages to people far away.

Check In | 1 | 2 | 3 | 4

Write Your Opinion

1 **Look** at your Build Knowledge pages in your reader's notebook. What did you learn about people working with animals?

2 **Write** your opinion. Which job working with animals is the most interesting? Include reasons for your opinion. Then compare your job with other jobs you read about. How are they alike and different? Use two vocabulary words from the Word Bank.

3 **Draw** a picture to go with your writing.

Think about what you learned this week. Fill in the bars on page 157.

Writing and Grammar

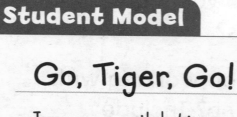
Steve

I wrote a poem about my favorite animal. My poem has rhythm and words that rhyme.

Student Model

Go, Tiger, Go!

I am a wild tiger,

I'm big and I'm strong,

My claws are sharp,

My tail is long!

Poem

My poem has rhythm. The words and syllables make a beat.

Ken Cavanagh/McGraw-Hill Education

Poem

My poem also has
words that rhyme.
They have the same
ending sounds.

I sleep in the day,

I hunt in the night,

Soon I will eat,

It's time for a bite!

Talk about what
makes Steve's writing
a poem.

Ask any questions you
have about the poem.

Circle the words
that rhyme.

Animals Everywhere **189**

Brainstorm and Plan

 Talk about animals you know.

Draw animals you might like to write about.

Quick Tip

You can use this sentence starter:

My favorite animals ...

Choose an animal to write about.

_____

- -

_____

_____

- -

Write what you know about the animal.

_____

- -

_____

_____

- -

_____

_____

- -

 Think about what words you might rhyme.

Writing and Grammar

Draft

Read Steve's draft of his poem.

Word Choice

My poem uses words that describe things.

Strong Verbs

I used strong verbs to describe actions.

Important Details

I included details in my poem.

> ### Student Model
>
> ## Go, Tiger, Go!
>
> I am a wild tiger,
>
> I'm big and I'm strong,
>
> I have claws,
>
> My tail is long!
>
> I sleep in the day, I hunt in the night,
>
> Soon I will eat, it's time for a bite!

Your Turn

Begin to write your poem in your Writer's Notebook. Use your ideas from pages 190–191. Use descriptive words and strong verbs.

Check In 1 2 3 4

Writing and Grammar

Revise and Edit

Think about how Steve revised and edited his poem.

Stanzas

I made my poem into two stanzas.

Student Model

Go, Tiger, Go!

I am a wild tiger,

I'm big and I'm strong,

My claws are sharp,

My tail is long!

I added details to make my poem more interesting.

Grammar

- Some verbs, such as *go*, have different forms in the present tense.
- Some verbs, such as *went*, have different forms in the past tense.
- Adverbs can tell when an action happens.

Line Breaks

I spelled a word with the long *e* sound correctly.

I used line breaks to show the rhythm of my poem.

I sleep in the day,

I hunt in the night,

Soon I will eat,

It's time for a bite!

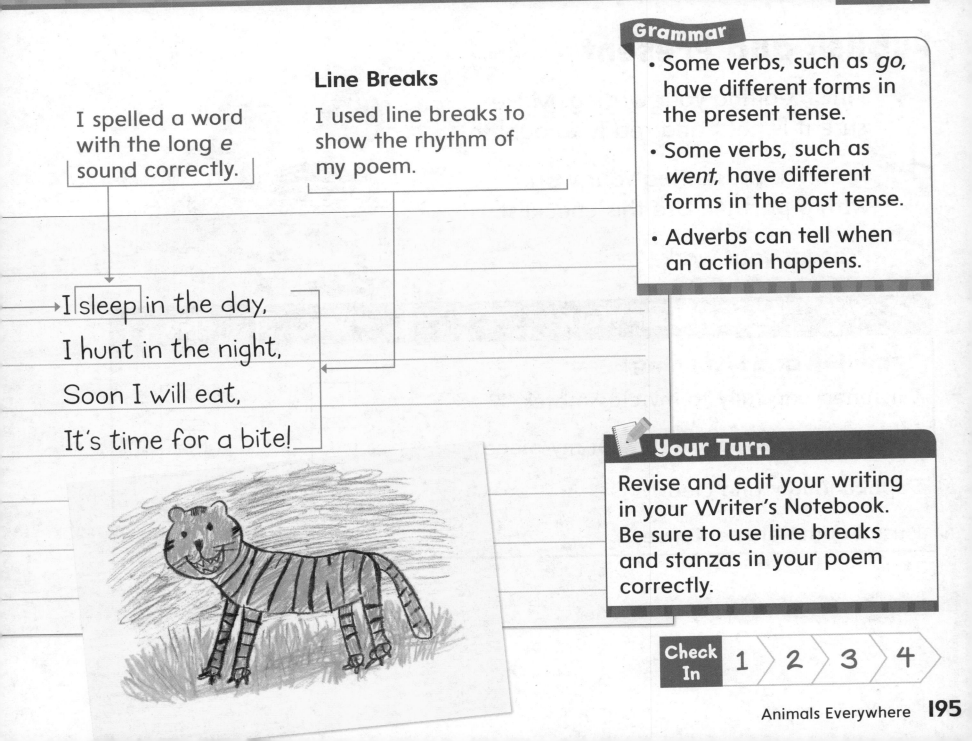

Your Turn

Revise and edit your writing in your Writer's Notebook. Be sure to use line breaks and stanzas in your poem correctly.

Check In 1 2 3 4

Publish and Present

 Finish editing your writing. Make sure it is neat and ready to publish.

 Practice presenting your work with a partner. Use this checklist.

Present your work.

Review Your Work	Yes	No
Speaking and Listening		
I listened carefully to my classmates.	☐	☐
I paid attention to the tone of my piece.	☐	☐
I spoke loudly and clearly.	☐	☐
I used complete sentences.	☐	☐

Talk with a partner about what you did well in your writing.

 What did you do well in your writing?

_____

_____

_____

_____

What do you need to work on?

_____

_____

_____

_____

 Think about your goal of writing a poem. Fill in the bars.

Check In 1 2 3 4

Connect to Science

My Goal
I can read and understand science texts.

 Find Text Evidence

 Ask yourself questions about the text. Read to find the answers.

Circle what crocodiles eat.

 Talk about what makes crocodiles special. Use details from the text.

Crocodiles

What animal lives on land and in water? A crocodile!

A crocodile's body helps it in many ways. Crocodiles live in warm wetlands. They have dull green skin. They use this as camouflage. It helps them blend in with grass and mud on land.

dull green skin

long, strong tail

A crocodile hides in water, too. Its eyes are on top of its head. It creeps into the water and peeks out to watch its surroundings.

Crocodiles have long, strong tails. This helps them run and swim very fast.

Crocodiles eat small prey, like fish and birds. They hide and wait until one swims or flies by. Then, when the moment is perfect, they strike!

Take Notes

Raymond Pauly/Shutterstock

Connect to Science

Ask yourself questions about the text. Read to find the answers.

Circle what sloths eat.

Talk about what makes sloths special. Use details from the text.

Sloths

What is one of the slowest animals on Earth? A sloth!

A sloth's body helps it in many ways. Sloths live in warm rain forests. They have strong arms. They have long, sharp claws, too. This helps them hold onto tree branches. They can hang for many days. A sloth spends most of its life upside down!

Sloths make homes in the trees. They get food from trees, too. Long claws help them pick leaves and fruit.

Sloths creep slowly through the trees. This helps them stay hidden from predators. They move so slowly, green algae grow on their backs. This helps sloths hide in leaves. The word "sloth" even means "slow!"

Hiding keeps sloths safe. They hide from animals like jaguars.

Take Notes

Compare the Passages

 Talk about how the texts "Crocodiles" and "Sloths" are the same and different.

 Compare how the animals in each text use their bodies to survive.

Crocodiles	Sloths

Write about how the animals in each text use their bodies to survive.

_____

- -

_____

- -

_____

- -

_____

- -

_____

- -

_____

Connect to Science

Observe Animal Needs

Talk about a new animal you would like to observe.

What to do

1. **Observe** an animal you can find near your school.

2. **Draw** a picture of your animal where it lives.

3. **Add** details and label the picture.

4. **Think** about where your animal lives. How does it help the animal?

5. **Write** about what you observed.

You need

pencil

crayons